DO MIRACLES HAPPEN?

Signs and Wonders in the Gospel of John

ISBN 978-1-949628-08-1
Printed in the United States of America.
10 9 8 7 6 5 4 3 2 1   22 21 20 19

Published by The Pastoral Center, http://pastoral.center.

Developed in partnership with MennoMedia and Brethren Press. Series editors: Fumiaki Tosu, Ann Naffziger, and Paul Canavese. *Do Miracles Happen?* Writer, Christy Risser. Project editor, Lani Wright. Staff editors, Susan E. Janzen, Julie Garber, and James Deaton. Updated design, Paul Stocksdale.

All rights reserved. Purchase of this book includes a license to reproduce this resource for use in a single parish, school, or other similar organization. You are allowed to share and make unlimited copies only for use within the organization that licensed it. If you serve more than one organization, each should purchase its own license. You may not post this document to any web site without explicit permission to do so. Outside of these conditions, no part of this book may be reproduced in any form or by any means, electronic or mechanical, including photocopying, recording, taping, or via any retrieval system, without the written permission of The Pastoral Center, 1212 Versailles Ave., Alameda, CA 94501. Thank you for cooperating with our honor system regarding our licenses.

For questions or to order additional copies or licenses, please call 1-844-727-8672 or visit http://pastoral.center.

Portions of this work © 2019 by The Pastoral Center / PastoralCenter.com. Adapted and published with permission from Generation Why Bible Studies. © 1996, 2014 Brethren Press, Elgin, IL 60120 and MennoMedia, Harrisonburg, VA 22803, U.S.A. All rights reserved.

Unless otherwise noted, the Scripture passages contained herein are from the *New Revised Standard Version of the Bible*, copyright © 1989 by the National Council of the Churches of Christ in the United States of America. Used by permission. All rights reserved.

Bible-based Explorations of Issues Facing Youth

>> OVERVIEW

When conversing online, the acronym IRL stands for "in real life." The virtual world of social media, text chats, blogs, and more have the power to remove us from the real world. What we experience online can skew our perspective on what it means to be human. It can numb us, incite us, distract us, depress us, confuse us, and make us rude or impatient. Strangely, this supposedly "social" and "connected" technology can profoundly disconnect us from others.

Religious faith can also place us in a bubble, especially when it distances us from others. When we keep the prophetic message at a safe distance, obscured in theological language and abstractions, we are missing the whole point. And when we see our parish as an insider club that serves itself, we can forget the radically inclusive message entrusted to us: God's love is for *everyone*, and God expects us to transform the *whole world* through that love.

Through the incarnation, God showed up in the real world to show us that our faith is not just about talking the talk, but also walking the walk. It can be risky. It can be confusing. It can hurt. But living out our faith can also bring us great purpose, peace, and joy.

This series connects the Bible with the tough questions that youth (and adults) encounter in their neighborhood, in school, among friends, and even online. This process will help you as a leader break open these issues in a fun and meaningful way, sparking conversation and the kind of life change Jesus invites us to embrace.

>> THE ROLE OF PARENTS

As children enter middle school and high school, they become more independent, self-reliant, and, well, self-centered. This can bring parents to make assumptions that this is the time to step back, giving their child more space to form their identity. While there is truth to that at some level (adolescents definitely shouldn't be smothered), this is a stage of life when parents should in fact *lean in*. The apparent confidence and bluster youth show on the outside can mask the insecurity and confusion on the inside. Youth need their parents to be involved more than ever.

>> WHOLE FAMILY FORMATION

Parents are the primary teachers of their own children, and parishes are waking up to the fact that faith formation programs need to bring parents into the process if they hope to see faith passed on to the next generation. Recent studies give us more and more evidence that the role of parents is the most important factor in determining whether a child will embrace faith as they move toward adulthood. Research from the Center for the Applied Research on the Apostolate shows that parents who talk about their faith and show through their actions that their faith is important to them are more likely to have children who remain Catholic.

More about Whole Family Formation »»»

To learn more about how your parish can take a comprehensive whole family approach to faith formation, visit **GrowingUpCatholic.com**.

While whole family events with elementary-aged children are on the rise, the role of parents can be an afterthought in youth ministry. We have designed the sessions in this series to work with or without parents present, and we encourage you to offer them as parent-child events.

If you choose to involve parents, it is important to consider before each session how to best do so. Many of the activities in this series are high-energy, creative, or silly. Some parents may need some encouragement to get out of their heads and have fun with the group. A few activities involving physical contact would be inappropriate for parents and youth to participate together, and we have noted them as such.

There are a number of ways to approach discussions with parent participation. Unless you have a small group, you will likely want to break into smaller groups for conversation. Some youth may be self-conscious and unable to be completely honest and open in a group situation with a parent present. For this reason, you may choose in some cases to assign parents to different groups from their own children, or to have separate parent and child groups altogether. Be sure to cover expectations around confidentiality. It is inappropriate for a parent (or youth) to share with another parent what their child said in a small group.

Note that even if parents and their children do not share all conversations together in the session, they will still have a valuable shared experience and can have extended conversations about it later.

» THANK YOU

The role you play in gathering, animating, praying with, and forming youth is a valuable one. Thank you for all you do to serve the church and its families!

Bible-based Explorations of Issues Facing Youth

>>> DO MIRACLES HAPPEN? <<<<<

Signs and Wonders in the Gospel of John

>>> INTRODUCTION

Are "signs of the times" visible today? Can we ourselves experience "miracles" like those in the Gospel of John? Not unless we approach the topic of miracles with hearts open to mystery and wonder in the realm of a living, active, loving God will we be able to.

The greatest miracle might be summed in John 1:14 and 3:16—the miracle of God's love that became flesh and lived among us. But John also included examples of what we more traditionally think of as miracles: the wonder of abundance from little; healing and restoration; signs of impossibility and faith; and the resurrection. In this particular Gospel, miracles are always referred to as "signs."

It is important in the beginning of this study to establish the role and purpose of signs in the Gospel of John. They point to the great act of the resurrection and the divinity of Jesus. It is from this backdrop that we must view the other signs and discover *why* they were performed. Then we can ask what they pointed to.

How does one *respond* to a miracle or a sign? One impulse is to try to reproduce it ourselves. But that's pushing God aside. The better response is to *follow the direction the sign is pointing to*, like the magi who followed the star to Jesus' crib. We will not necessarily answer all the questions, but we will wrestle with the possibilities. Sometimes, the greatest learning comes not from finding answers, but in struggling with the questions themselves. In examining the possibilities, we may find miracles we overlook every day. Looking at not only the wondrous signs themselves, but also examining the *why* behind Jesus' use of these signs will be what we explore through this unit.

In the end, either you are open to belief that Jesus performed miracles, or you aren't. There isn't much room for a middle ground. And it can be very scary to come face-to-face with a sign pointing to the living God, a miracle. From C. S. Lewis' classic, *Miracles*:

> It is always shocking to meet life where we thought we were alone. "Look out!" we cry, "it's **alive**." And therefore this is the very point at which so many draw back...and proceed no further with Christianity. An "impersonal God"—well and good. A subjective God of beauty, truth and goodness, inside our own heads—better still. A formless life-force surging through us, a vast power which we can tap—best of all. But God ... alive, pulling at the other end of the cord...that is quite another matter....

>>>

"Those who assume that miracles cannot happen are merely wasting their time by looking into the texts: we know in advance what results they will find for they have begun by begging the question."

C. S. Lewis, *Miracles*

EXTENDER SESSION

Extender sessions suggest special activities related to the issue of the unit. They help accommodate the diversity of parish schedules. Since each unit is undated, youth may study units in their entirely and still participate in special events of the parish that get scheduled simultaneously with youth group time. Extender sessions can be used anytime, but the one for this unit best follows **Session 2 (*Option A*)** or **Session 3 (*Option B*)**. Calculate now whether or not you will be using the extender session.

*So it is a sort of Rubicon. One goes across; or not. But if one does, there is no manner of security against miracles. One may be in for **anything**.*

PREPARATION ALERT

Responding to a miracle or sign starts with prayer; each of the Respond sections of this unit will involve praying the miracle/sign highlighted in the session. Prayer is available at all times, not just to ask for hearts to see miracles, but to invite God's presence into the situation.

You may wish to set aside a corner of the room, a sort of prayer closet, especially for this time during each session. Use a privacy screen, or even move to another room, a chapel perhaps. Try to create an atmosphere conducive of prayer.

Be aware, too, that an option in Session 3 depends on arranging with the pastor to come into your meeting to talk with the group about healing.

THE TEACHING PLAN: The parts of the session guide

Faith story. The session is rooted in this Bible passage.

Faith focus. The story of the passage in a nutshell.

Session goal. The entire session is built around this goal. What changes—in knowledge, attitude, and/or action—do you desire in your group?

Materials needed and advance preparation. This is what you will need if the session is to go smoothly. You'll feel more at ease if you've taken care of these details before you meet your group.

FROM LIFE TO BIBLE TO LIFE

The teaching plan we use is called *life-centered*. However, when we write each session, we always begin with scripture. We ask, what does this particular passage say, especially to youth? Each session moves from life to Bible to life. So the Bible is really at the center of this way of teaching.

In every session we try to hit upon a tough question that youth might ask. Find out what questions on this issue are important for your group. Feel free to bring your own input and invite your group members to add their own experiences.

❯❯ TEACHING THE SESSION

The five step-by-step movements will carry you from *life to the Bible and back to life*. Each session takes about 45 to 50 minutes. If there is a handout sheet for the session, take note of any complementary activities and stories.

1. **Focus.** Intended to create a friendly climate within the group and to *draw attention* to the issue.

2. **Connect.** Invites participants to *express* their own life experience about the issue, through talking, drawing, role playing, and other activities. Also use memory, reason, or imagination to get the group thinking about *why* they view the issue the way they do.

3. **Explore the Bible.** What does the Bible say about the issue? With a minimum of lecturing, dig into the faith story and search for answers to questions raised in the first activities. The Insights from Scripture section will help clarify the faith story. Help participants discover how the faith community understands the Bible passage.

4. **Apply** the faith story. What does the Bible passage *mean* for contemporary life? This is the "aha!" moment when participants realize the faith story has wisdom for *their* lives.

5. **Respond.** Why does the Bible passage *matter*? What will the group do about the issue in light of what they have learned from their own experiences set alongside the faith story? How can we *live* the faith story rather than pass it off as a mere intellectual exercise?

❯❯ LOOK AHEAD

Here are reminders for what you need to do for the next session or two.

❯❯ INSIGHTS FROM SCRIPTURE

Here is a resource for Explore the Bible. Don't try to use all the material given. Take what you need to lead the session and answer questions your group may have. Let the Insights section inspire you to think and study more about the passage for the session.

❯❯ HANDOUT SHEETS

Occasionally, there will be a handout sheet to complement your session. If you choose to use this, make enough copies for the group in advance of the session. These sheets may include questions, stories, agree/disagree exercises, charts, pictures, and other materials to stimulate thinking and discussion.

Generally, no participant preparation is required unless the session plan calls for you to contact selected group members for specific tasks.

SESSION 1

TALES OF WONDER... FACT OR FICTION?

KEY VERSE

"For God so loved the world that he gave his only Son, so that everyone who believes in him may not perish but may have eternal life." (John 3:16)

FAITH STORY

John 3:1-17

FAITH FOCUS

Nicodemus, a Jewish theologian, went to Jesus trying to find out for himself who Jesus was. In the Gospel of John, all "signs" that Jesus performed had to do with revealing who Jesus is, the Son of God. These signs and tales of wonder point to the miracle of incarnation—God sending Jesus into the world.

SESSION GOAL

Help participants establish the role of signs in the Gospel of John, so they can begin to redefine what to expect from a miracle—a sign of God's presence in our world.

TEACHING PLAN

Materials needed and advance preparation

- Box of wooden matches, 15 for every two people in the group (*Option A* in Focus)
- Video camera and media player (*Option B* in Focus)
- Chalkboard/chalk or newsprint/marker
- Copies of the handout sheet for Session 1 (*Option C* in Focus)
- Bibles
- Writing paper/pencils
- Kitchen timer

1. FOCUS 12-15 minutes

Option A: Many a Miss. Pair up. Each set of players lays out 15 matches in a row. Players decide who goes first, and then take turns picking up 1, 2, or 3 matches at a time, until they are all gone. The object of the game is to *avoid* picking up the last match; that is, to force the opponent to do it.

Tip *(but don't give it out!):* In order to ensure picking up the 14th match, the 10th match must be taken, so players must count carefully.

Play a few rounds, then ask: *Is this a game of chance? Is it a game of probability? Is it a game of skill?* Point out that different people may also see miracles in this light: a chance, a probability (associated with scientific theory), or feats of skill or trickery.

>>> **Option B:** Reporter on the Street. Interview people, asking, *What is a sign, biblically speaking, that is?* As you make note of the responses, get as creative as you like, perhaps even video-recording responses of people not only in the study group, but also of others in the faith community. If you choose to interview others before meeting time, make sure a media player and screen are available for playback. If you wish to do this with just your group, ask each one to write or draw answers on a chalkboard or newsprint. Review the responses.

>>> **Option C:** Divide into two groups, the **realists** and the **dreamers**. (These divisions need not apply to the actual mental state of the participants.) Distribute copies of the handout sheet. The realists will argue that miracles may have happened in Jesus' time, but do not and probably cannot happen today. They must present convincing evidence in favor of their position. The dreamers will present the opposing side: that miraculous events happen every day in our world, and were not just a phenomenon of Jesus' day. They argue that the reason the realists do not see miracles is because they either do not want to, or they just don't know where to look. Allow 10 minutes for preparation, and each side two minutes to present. Follow up the debate with a discussion of which side seemed more convincing, and why. Also discuss whether the titles "realists" and "dreamers" were appropriate. Should the realists have been the ones who argued that miracles are a reality? Use a chalkboard or newsprint to keep track of relevant points.

> "The logical man must either deny all miracles or none."
>
> Charles Alexander Eastman (Native American writer and physician, 1858-1939)

2. CONNECT 6-8 minutes

Explore attitudes about miracles by relating the following scenario:

> *Some scientists in a rural town managed to make it possible for a cow to be able to carry a human fetus to term. In other words, cows were giving birth to human babies (with a lot of help from some test tubes and scientists sporting long rubber gloves). At least one teenage girl, Kimberly, experienced a definite crisis of faith because of this. She even tells her youngest brother that there probably is no God and miracles don't happen.*
>
> *Their mother, a physician, overhears this and wants to know why she doesn't believe in God or miracles anymore. Kimberly tells her that there's no sense of wonder in the world anymore. Babies are grown inside of cows. Scientists disprove things that were always thought of as miraculous every day. There's no reason to believe in anything, because there isn't anything to believe in.*

Now ask:

- Do you agree with Kimberly? Why or why not?
- It's true that scientists discover more and more every day about the universe. How do you think these discoveries affect your feelings about the miraculous?
- How do they affect your experience of God's presence in the world today?

> "There are only two ways to live your life. One is as though nothing is a miracle. The other is as though everything is a miracle."
>
> Albert Einstein (German-born theoretical physicist, 1879-1955)

3. EXPLORE THE BIBLE 8 minutes

Shift to this activity by saying: *In a world where we're taught that anything not proved in the laboratory is merely speculation, believing in the miraculous is tough. John's Gospel shows us signs and tales of wonder that point to the miracle of God sending Jesus into our world.*

Distribute Bibles and read John 3:1-17. Give a mini-lecture (no more than 5 minutes) based on information provided in the Insights from Scripture section, allowing room for unique and applicable responses from the group. Explain how and why John emphasized signs in his Gospel. Point out how John is different from the other three Gospels. His purpose was to show how the things Jesus said and did all pointed to who he was: God's Son. Looking at not only the wondrous signs themselves, but also examining the *why* behind Jesus' use of these signs will be what we explore through this unit.

4. APPLY 5-6 minutes

Pair up, and hand out paper and pencils. Set the timer, and tell participants they have 1 minute to write down **everything they know about God**. Remind them that what they know about *Jesus* gives us clues as to who God is. When a minute is up, have one pair read their list. If any other pair lists that same thing, they cancel each other out. Any unique answers must be accompanied by an explanation: *How* do they know that about God?

Tip: Participants will likely write concrete things: loving, generous, etc. Point out that the miracles Jesus performed tell us who God (and Jesus) is.

5. RESPOND 8-10 minutes

How does one *respond* to a miracle or a sign? One response is to try to reproduce it ourselves. But that's pushing God aside. The better response is to *follow the direction the sign is pointing to*, like the magi who followed the star to Jesus' crib. Following God-in-Jesus starts with prayer; each of the Respond sections of this unit will involve praying the miracle/sign highlighted in the session. Prayer is available at all times, not just to ask for miracles, but to invite God's presence into the situation.

You may wish to set aside a corner of the room, a sort of prayer closet, especially for this time during each session. Use a privacy screen, or even move to another room, a chapel perhaps. Try to create an atmosphere of prayer.

Pray the miracle. Move to your prayer space. First, read John 3:1-17 again. Then ask participants to close their eyes and try to see themselves in each of the characters of the Bible passage (go slowly): Nicodemus, Jesus, Moses lifting the serpent so that the people bitten by snakes might live (Num. 21:8), the people who were bitten (i.e., the hurting world).

Next, read again (slowly) John 3:17: "Indeed, God did not send the Son into the world to condemn the world, but in order that the world might be saved through him."

Next (with eyes still closed), name each person in the room in turn. As you speak the names, ask participants to think of that person as the image of God. Because they are created in the image of God, this person has the capability to help us know who God is! Finally, end with the benediction suggested below, or depart in a way you choose.

Suggested benediction: Be miracles yourselves—signs of God's presence in the world.

INSIGHTS FROM SCRIPTURE

John's Gospel takes a different approach to the idea of signs (miracles) than do any of the other three Gospels. In fact, John takes a different approach to the entire story of Jesus. None of the signs (a.k.a. miracles) in the Gospel of John can ever be seen separately from the Son of God, Jesus. Every one of the signs in John has to do with revealing who Jesus is. John is not particularly concerned with the actual events, spectacular though some of them may be. John's concern is communicating that Jesus is the Son of the one and only God, and that the one and only God sent Jesus here to save us from ourselves.

John 3:16 is one of the most oft-quoted verses in the Bible. During the Reformation in the 16th century, Martin Luther (the man credited with starting the Reformation) made a powerful statement about this verse. He said that it contains the entire gospel story in just those few words. "For God so loved the world that he gave his only Son, so that everyone

"Jesus' self-revelation in John is actually the whole of his 'ministry.' Everything he says and does is calculated to make known to potential disciples who he is, where he comes from, and who it is who sent him."

Sandra Schneiders, I.H.M., *Written that You May Believe*

LOOK AHEAD

For next session, you'll need food and drink for a "communion lunch" (see Apply).

> **In the Gospel of John, Jesus' miracles and words point us to who Jesus is, and where he comes from—the bosom of God.**
>
> Sandra Schneiders, I.H.M., paraphrased from *Written that You May Believe*

who believes in him may not perish, but may have eternal life." Just that first clause is amazing. God loves us, and loves us so much that Jesus, the Word of God, became flesh and lived among us (John 1:14). As Madeleine L'Engle writes, "The first of the gloriously impossible things that Jesus did was to be born—the power that created the universe come to live with us as one of us."

These verses are not typically seen as a part of a miracle story, but consider the possibility. What a great miracle that God could love us so much! What a great miracle that the Word of God became flesh and *lived among us*.

In the Gospel of John, the writer consistently uses the verb "give" to describe God as the source of what Jesus offers the world. Jesus "gives" humans the opportunity to experience redemption and reconciliation with God. Jesus "gives" of himself to bring humanity into right relationship with God. But verse 16 is the only place in the Gospel of John where it says that God "gave" Jesus to us humans. John typically uses the verb "sent." In other words, God is the source of Jesus. John wants to make sure in verse 16 that no one can mistake the origins of Jesus.

Another unique characteristic of verse 16 is the use of the word "world." God gave Jesus to the "world." John frequently uses the word "world" to refer to a specific group of people within humanity. Those at odds with God are the "world." It could be argued that we are all at odds with God, but John was pointing particularly to the Gentiles who worshiped false gods instead of the one true God. John takes much time throughout his Gospel emphasizing that Jesus came to the Gentiles, those who were not considered "chosen people."

›› THE SEEKERS

In verses 1-21, John uses the example of Nicodemus to move from a general overview of God's creation to the specific individual. Nicodemus symbolizes each of our individual hearts seeking God. Nicodemus sought out Jesus. This, for John, is the first sign of discipleship. But there was a catch. "[Nicodemus] came to Jesus by night and said to him, 'Rabbi, we know that you are a teacher who has come from God; for no one can do these signs that you do apart from the presence of God.'" John portrayed Nicodemus seeking Jesus at *night* instead of during the day. One could say that Nicodemus did this to avoid detection or ridicule from Jews, but John may have had a different idea in mind. Nighttime is often used in the Bible as a metaphor for separation from God. Throughout Job, Proverbs, the Psalms, and even the Gospels, the darkness is the place where there is "weeping and gnashing of teeth." Nicodemus may have come to Jesus seeking a right relationship with God, but was not immediately willing to commit all he was and all he had to his search. He came under darkness of night, hoping to see if Jesus was indeed the real thing.

Youth today may feel the same way, with some resisting even looking in the very place that describes Jesus best: the Bible. They have yet to be convinced that the Bible is a worthwhile read, that it has any authority. In his Gospel, John was out to establish authority, the first step in gaining credibility. He was bent on establishing the authority of Jesus as God's Son, so people would want to respond to him. In that motive lie all the miracles and signs described by John.

TALES OF WONDER... FACT OR FICTION?

In Real Life — Exploring tough questions facing youth today

>>> "The logical man must either deny all miracles or none."

Charles Alexander Eastman (Native American writer and physician, 1858-1939)

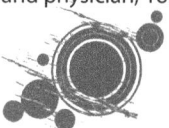

Debate: You have been selected to active membership in a group whose view you may or may not believe. Still, you and your group will come up with convincing arguments to support your point of view. You will have about 10 minutes to prepare, then each group will have two minutes to present. Feel free to use props, personal experience, quotes, or instant video, if you have Internet access.

Are you a REALIST?

Your group will argue that miracles may have happened in Jesus' time, but do not and probably cannot happen today. What convincing points will you make to support this position?

OR a DREAMER?

You will present evidence that miraculous events happen every day in our world, and were not just a phenomenon of Jesus' day. The reason the realists do not see miracles is because they either do not want to, or they just don't know where to look.

>>> "There are only two ways to live your life. One is as though nothing is a miracle. The other is as though everything is a miracle."

Albert Einstein (German-born theoretical physicist, 1879-1955)

After the debate, discuss which side seemed more convincing, and why. Also discuss whether the titles "realists" and "dreamers" were appropriate. Should the realists have been the ones who argued that miracles are a reality?

Do Miracles Happen? : Session 1

Permission is granted to photocopy this handout for use with this session.

>>> **SESSION 2**

A FREE LUNCH? >>>

>> KEY VERSES

When he looked up and saw a large crowd coming toward him, Jesus said to Philip, "Where are we to buy bread for these people to eat?" He said this to test him, for he himself knew what he was going to do. (John 6:5-6)

>> FAITH STORY

John 6:1-15

>> FAITH FOCUS

In feeding the 5,000, Jesus fulfilled a physical need of people who also had hungry souls. Jesus' grace is shown through a physical, tangible gift. The key was for the recipients of that grace (here, the bread and fish) to recognize that this good gift was from God through Jesus.

>> SESSION GOAL

Lead participants in discovering what Jesus' "physical" signs say about God: that God cares for our physical as well as our spiritual needs.

>> Materials needed and advance preparation

- Set up start and finish lines (*Option A* in Focus)
- Chalkboard/chalk or newsprint/marker
- Copies of the handout sheet for Session 2
- Bibles
- Food and drink for a "communion lunch" (see Apply)

 **TEACHING PLAN**

1. FOCUS 10-12 minutes

>> **Option A:** (for large groups, camp, or retreat setting): Divide into teams of no less than five, making the teams even as possible. Set up a starting line and a finish line that are approximately 25 feet apart. Tell participants that the task is to get their team from the start to the finish with as few body parts touching the ground as is possible. The winners are the team to finish the race with the fewest body parts touching the ground.

Like Jesus' feeding of the 5,000, this is a *physical challenge*. It also requires some creativity in building. The team must move as a single unit. Hands, knees, and feet each count separately. Body parts dragging on the floor also must be included in the count.

In Real Life | Do Miracles Happen?   15

>>>
Tests for a "real" miracle, according to theology professor J. Rodman Williams:

1. **It glorifies God.** Miracles always declare that God is active in our world...The principal test of any miracle—then, now, or in the future—is this: Who receives the glory?
2. **It stems from a righteous source.**
3. **It rings true to the Holy Spirit.**
4. **It stands the test of external verification.**
5. **It builds up the church.**

>> **Option B:** Say: *Imagine you are going on a 4-day wilderness survival hike. No grocery stores, no trash cans, no vending machines, no coffeepots, no pack animals. What food do you **really** need to take along? What are your calorie needs for 4 days of strenuous exercise?* Work together to compile a pack list for one person. Write the list on chalkboard or newsprint. If you have it, use the Internet to find tips (such as http://sectionhiker.com/3-day-backpacking-menu/, http://www.backpacking.net/27-pound.html#food, or http://www.backpacker.com/skills/beginner/backpacking-101/) to supplement common knowledge within the group.

2. CONNECT 8 minutes

Gather the whole group on one side of the room (if you're outside, one knot of people). Call out the following physical descriptions. Anyone who fits the description must go to the other side of the room and play **one round** of Ring Around the Rosey (singing is mandatory!).

- Wears glasses or contacts
- Has two left feet (is clumsy)
- Has a scar
- Has a dimple
- Drinks coffee regularly
- Had to eat in the past 24 hours

By the time you get to the last one, it will be easy to point out that everyone has some sort of physical need or idiosyncrasy.

3. EXPLORE THE BIBLE 15-18 minutes

Shift to this activity by saying: *Everyone has some sort of physical challenge every day, even if it's only to make sure their belly gets filled. Jesus' disciples one day found themselves with a big physical challenge: how to feed over 5,000 people with just a little fish and bread. It would take a miracle. Or maybe it was a sign....*

Distribute copies of the handout sheet, and recruit volunteers for the skit scripted there.

After the skit, have everyone return to their places. Pass out Bibles and have everyone use John 6:1-15 as a reference as you discuss the following questions. Allow discussion of each question before offering the answer.

1. *Why do you think Jesus would ask Philip how to feed the crowd if he already had in mind how to do it?*

Answer: Jesus was constantly questioning the disciples to find out how much they really understood what he was all about. He also asked them questions to make them think. Philip had seen Jesus perform other great acts by this time, so why would he not automatically think that Jesus could take care of feeding these people? Most likely it was because he and the other disciples had a real problem with thinking beyond the human situation to the realm of God.

2. *Even though it wasn't in the skit, the Bible says there were twelve baskets of food left over from the feast. Why did Jesus make too much?*

Answer: This miracle wasn't just about feeding the hungry people who were following Jesus. It was about the truly abundant life Jesus provides for those who are faithful to his call. Also, the words Jesus uses in verse 12 are unique to John's version of this story. Those words may be relating this story of feeding back to the story of God feeding the Israelites with manna in the desert (Exodus 16). Moses asked the people not to leave the manna lying around, and when they did, God allowed the manna to get really disgusting with worms and a bad smell.

Later verses in this chapter (vv. 25-59) confirm the relationship to the manna story is very important for John.

> **3.** *In verse 14, the people confess that Jesus is a prophet. In verse 15, it says that they intended to make him a king. Why do you think Jesus rejected this honor?*

Answer: The two events are related. The people were making a confession about the nature of Jesus based on a physical act. They didn't really understand who Jesus is. They saw that he had fed them, and they declared him a prophet and wanted to make him king because he fed them. Jesus *is* a king, but not in a worldly sense. The crowd did not understand that, just as they did not understand the power Jesus used to feed them.

4. APPLY 10-12 minutes

Because of this story's connection to the communion (Eucharist) celebrations of the early church, you may find it appropriate to have an agape meal with your group. It also highlights the point that God provides for our physical as well as our spiritual needs. Try a simple, but unconventional, food and/or drink that emphasizes the "making do with what you have" nature of the story—crackers or bagels or bread, and water or juice boxes—things that remind one of lunch on the journey.

Have participants share this agape meal with each other in a circle (no more than 5-8 in one circle). As an option for passing the "feast" to each other, have them say to their neighbor, *Jesus feeds us with love and bread.*

5. RESPOND 8-12 minutes

Move to your "prayer closet" area.

Pray the miracle. First, ask participants to close their eyes and try to see themselves in each of the characters of the story for this session (go slowly): Philip (who wondered how on earth he was going to get the bread), Jesus, Andrew (who found the boy with the food), the boy who was asked to share his food, the hungry people, the disciples (who gathered up the leftover food).

Suggested benediction: God cares for us, both our physical and our spiritual needs. Thanks be to God!

>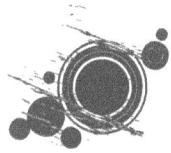
> "Miracles happen. But prayer is needed! Prayer that is courageous, struggling and persevering, not prayer that is a mere formality."
>
> Pope Francis, May 2013

INSIGHTS FROM SCRIPTURE

Note: Much of the information that would normally go in this section is in the Explore the Bible section of this session.

This miracle is the only one found in all four Gospels, although each tells it a bit differently. This is a clue that this event was likely one of the more popular stories of Jesus to be passed along in the early church. One of the reasons for its popularity is that, in a way, it symbolizes the Eucharist (communion) celebration for the early church.

John tells the actual miracle with fewer words than the other Gospels. Again, the event itself is not the point for John. That is why, though it is a laudable project, running out to feed the hungry in response to this miracle misses the point. Instead, the point is who this event shows Jesus to be. Jesus is the Messiah. John knew this when he was writing the story, and so allowed this knowledge to fill each event he recorded in his Gospel.

»» LOOK AHEAD

The next session would be a good time for the Extended Session, *Option A*. If not, arrange with the pastor to come into your meeting to talk with the group about the topic of healing in your parish. See Session 3: Apply, *Option B*.

»» WHO'S THE CHEF?

When Jesus asked Philip how they were going to feed the large crowd, John is working at an important point. The identity of Jesus as the Christ is extremely important in the whole of the Gospel of John. If the disciples recognized the source of the gifts of Jesus, then they would come closer to recognizing the true identity of Jesus. Neither of the disciples mentioned in the passage could answer Jesus' question. They thought of the question in its literal sense, and not as a question Jesus was asking about himself. Traditional thinking cannot comprehend what Jesus has to offer, much less what he is about to do in the story. Jesus is the only one who knows how to meet the needs of the crowd on this day.

In the other Gospel accounts of this miracle, the disciples distributed the food that Jesus provided (Matt 14:19; Mark 6:41; Luke 9:16). In John, however, Jesus is the one who distributes the food (verse 11). This, again, is John pointing to Jesus as the Christ, the one who gives the abundant goodness to God's people.

This story is not a directive to Christians to feed the multitudes. It is a story about who Jesus is, and thus who God is, and how God shows love: by fulfilling physical needs as well as spiritual needs. When we *follow* Jesus, we try to emulate the ways he loved. Only then do we become compelled to meet needs in the way Jesus did.

Jesus Feeds Us with Love and Bread

Note: Feel free to fill these "male" roles with females.

JESUS: *(standing, looking out over an imaginary crowd)* Philip! Hey, Philip! Over here!

PHILIP: *(enters and comes over to where Jesus is sitting)* Yeah? What's up?

JESUS: You see all of these people out here, right? *(Philip nods.)* How many of them do you think there are?

PHILIP: I have no idea. But I think Andrew was counting them not too long ago. *(looks around for Andrew)* There he is. *(shouts)* Hey Andrew! Come over here a sec.

ANDREW: *(enters)* Yeah, what can I do for you?

JESUS: Andrew, do you know how many people are out there?

ANDREW: I just finished counting, and there are about 4,000 men in the crowd.

JESUS: What about women and children? How many of them are there?

PHILIP: *(not happy)* You want us to go back and count the women and children, too?

JESUS: No, that's not necessary, I just wondered.

ANDREW: Well, if you count women and children, there are probably over 8,000 people here today. Why do you ask?

JESUS: Philip, where can we buy enough bread for these people to eat?

PHILIP: *(shocked)* Jesus, if we were to clean out every store in a day's walk from here there still wouldn't be enough for everyone to eat! Not to mention the fact that we'd never be able to pay for all of the food, even if we could get it.

ANDREW: Almost no one brought food with them, either. I found a boy with five loaves of barley bread and two fish, but what difference does that make in a crowd this size?

JESUS: *(thinks for just a moment)* Philip, why don't you and the others get the crowd to sit down and be still. *(Philip nods and exits.)* Andrew, do you think you can find that boy and bring him to me?

ANDREW: I guess. *(looks around)* There he is. *(shouts)* You there, boy! Yes, you. Come here please. Jesus would like to speak with you.

BOY: *(enters carrying a small bag with something in it)* Yes, sir. You called?

JESUS: What is your name?

BOY: Noah.

JESUS: *(smiles)* Well, Noah, Andrew here tells me that you have some bread and fish with you today. Is that true?

BOY: Yes, sir. I do.

JESUS: Noah, would you allow me to use your bread and fish to feed this crowd *(indicates crowd as he's saying it)*?

BOY: *(wide-eyed at the size of the crowd)* Sir, how can my loaves and fish feed all of these people? It's barely enough for me!

JESUS: *(laughs)* That's because you're still growing. I can do it, Noah. I can feed all of these people with only your loaves and fish.

BOY: *(suspiciously)* How?

JESUS: Do you believe in God, Noah? *(Noah nods.)* Well then, do you believe that God can do anything? *(Noah nods again.)* What would you say if I told you that I can do anything that God can do?

BOY: I don't know.

JESUS: **How about if you trust me and we'll see?**

BOY: Okay. *(He hands over the small bag he was carrying to Jesus and exits.)*

(Jesus exits. End of skit.)

>>> SESSION 3

FAITH, HEALING, AND PRAYER >>>

>>> KEY VERSE

Jesus asked, "Won't any of you believe in me unless I do more and more miracles?" (John 4:48, TLB)

>>> FAITH STORY

John 4:46-53

>>> FAITH FOCUS

A royal official came to Jesus and asked him to heal his child. Though Jesus gave him a bit of a rough time about it, he nonetheless sent the man home with the assurance that the child would be healed. On his way home, the man met a servant who confirmed the promise Jesus made. The official's son was alive and well, and the healing came at precisely the time Jesus had spoken the words. Can people today be healed by faith and prayer? What about those who aren't healed with prayer? Do they not have enough faith?

>>> SESSION GOAL

Help participants wrestle with the purpose of prayer and faith in terms of healing, seeing Jesus as the Giver of life, not a magician.

>>> Materials needed and advance preparation

- Bibles
- Chalkboard/chalk or newsprint/marker
- Copies of the handout sheet for Session 3
- Arrange with the pastor to talk with the group about healing (*Option B* in Apply)

TEACHING PLAN

1. FOCUS 3 MINUTES

Tell the following true story:

> *There was once a young woman who was terribly injured in a car crash that was not her fault. She recovered, but was confined to a wheelchair. She was nonetheless in good spirits, and was courageous enough to stay very active. She traveled to other countries, went camping with friends, lived in her own apartment, and took part in church activities. She was a loving and generous soul, but she still wanted so badly to walk again. She prayed for healing, and her friends prayed with her.*

> *She announced one day that God had told her she would be able to walk unaided up a short staircase in her apartment. This great event was to happen at 6 p.m. on Thursday of the next week. She invited all her friends to her apartment that night, and they ate together, and prayed together for this healing. The anticipation mounted as the clock drew closer to 6.*
>
> *Finally, the woman rolled her chair to the stairs, and pushed herself up and out, grabbing for the railing to steady herself. Her friends gathered in a tight circle behind her for spiritual support, but did not lay hands on her, because she was determined to walk the stairs unaided. But instead of climbing the stairs, the young woman collapsed in a heap. She struggled up four times, and four times her legs gave way beneath her. She did not walk the stairs.*

»» GRAPPLING WITH FAITH AND HEALING...

An 11-year-old with diabetes died because his mother refused medical treatment and tried instead to treat him with prayer. When his father, who was divorced from the mother, sued, the courts awarded him $1.5 million in damages. Some Christian groups, whether or not they agree with the mother's methods, believe the ruling may lead to other "clergy malpractice" suits. A representative of the Baptist Joint Committee explained, "When it comes to spiritual things such as the quality and reasonableness of prayer and healing, courts should not be involved."

Headline news

2. CONNECT 10-12 minutes

Form a circle with chairs. If your group is especially big, make several circles. The key is to create a comfortable space for talking. Ask participants to consider the following two questions.

1. *Who have you known that has suffered horribly or died, even though you or others were praying for their recovery?*
2. *What do you do about suffering that happens, even when we are promised in the Bible that prayer and asking God can and does heal people?*

Suggest that they tell their stories quickly and focus primarily on the second question. Emphasize that there are no right or wrong answers. This could be a touchy subject with some. Experiencing human suffering is difficult and complex. Some may question God's motives and sometimes even God's presence. This is normal. Handle with care.

3. EXPLORE THE BIBLE 10-12 minutes

Shift to this activity by saying: *Jesus was constantly faced with people expecting him to perform miracles for them. They expected miracles to heal them. What they learned is that miracles reveal who Jesus is.*

Choose one of the following options for hearing the story of the healing of the royal official's son. One option is for groups who are familiar with many Bible stories, and the other is for groups that are fairly new to the stories. **The questions following are for both options.** Ask someone to distribute Bibles as you write the questions on the chalkboard or newsprint. These are not easy questions, and they don't have obvious answers.

» **Option A:** Have someone read John 4:46- 53, and have the rest of the group listen for possible answers to the questions. (The answers are simply guides to help if people get stuck. Encourage attempts to answer the questions, sort of like code-breakers, and not give up quickly just because they are difficult.)

» **Option B:** Ask one person to start telling the story of the royal official's son, without looking at the passage. The person who can identify the first error or omission becomes the new storyteller. Repeat this sequence until the entire story has been told. Challenge participants to try the same thing again, using a modern-day setting. Then discuss the questions below.

1. *Which government did this official most likely work for?*

Answer: The official was in the employ of Rome. John calls him a "royal official." That is a fairly ambiguous title, but may have referred to a tax collector or a secretary under the governor of the province.

2. *Why would he come to Jesus to help his son?*

Answer: This is an interesting question, because if the man was indeed Roman, he had a great many gods to turn to for help for his child. In fact, this man had probably spent a lot of time and money in trying to get his child healed in the temples of any number of gods. Obviously, the methods didn't work.

It is likely that in that part of the country, Jesus' turning the water into wine had become something of a great news story. If the official had heard about Jesus turning water into wine and realized that the Roman gods were not going to help his child, he would have turned to anyone, and Jesus would have been a possible choice.

3. *Why would the official have taken Jesus' word for it when Jesus said that his son was healed?*

Answer: Remember, Jesus was just some guy wandering the countryside, talking about God and love and doing the occasional miracle. At this time, he was not widely considered to be the Messiah. But perhaps the official sensed the special authority of Jesus, and could not help but believe. Perhaps the Spirit came upon the man and convicted him of the truth of Jesus' words. Perhaps he only hoped that Jesus was telling the truth and wanted to head home as quickly as possible to see if it was true.

4. *Other than the fact that the healing helped a sick person and his family, what other reasons could Jesus have had for performing this miracle?*

Answer: This, as with all of the miracles in the Gospel of John, is intended to point ahead to the identity of Jesus. It is never just the simple act of healing with Jesus. Look at the end of the story. What happens to the royal official when he discovers that what Jesus said actually happened? He and his household came to faith in Jesus as the Messiah. John is trying to convert his readers. John wants people to come to faith in Jesus. He is showing us here that Jesus healed people, even from afar, so we should believe him to be the Messiah. Remember that John knows the end of the gospel story as he is writing this story of the royal official's son. He knows that Jesus is the Messiah. He wants everyone else to know that, too. That is why he wrote down this miracle.

4. APPLY 10 minutes

Option A: Use the short writing on the handout sheet to jumpstart thinking about how God surprises us by being present, even when it may not be immediately apparent that God is with us. Read the piece aloud, and slowly, to the group before passing out the handout sheets for them to take with them.

Make the point that, when things look bleak or healing seems impossible, we may need to look at the problem from a different angle, or from a different time frame, to see God's presence. (**Note:** Though the words "lucky" and "unlucky" are used, think of God's presence being involved, in order to make your point.)

Option B: Arrange with the pastor to come into your meeting to converse with the group about the way in which the church uses a healing scripture like this. Encourage participants to question the pastor about the role of miraculous healings in your parish, or the lack of healing there. What does your pastor feel is the most biblical way of dealing with sickness and pain within your congregation? Does your pastor have any suggestions for what your group can do to explore the topic of healing further if they would be interested?

> "We are living in a world that is absolutely transparent, and God is shining through it all the time. This is not just a fable or a nice story, it is true... If we abandon ourselves to God and forget ourselves we see... that God manifests Himself everywhere, in everything.."
>
> Thomas Merton
> *Essential Writings*

LOOK AHEAD

The next session would be a good time for the Extended Session, *Option B*. If not, prepare several pieces of paper with ink blots or crayon blots. See Session 4: Focus, Option A.

> It is God's presence in Jesus' acts that makes them become signs, pointing to something beyond the miraculous act itself. God's presence in the acts of Jesus holds together the physical and the spiritual. It is evidence that Jesus is the "Word made flesh."

5. RESPOND 8-10 minutes

Move to your "prayer closet" area.

Pray the miracle. First, ask people to close eyes and try to see themselves in each of the characters of the story (go slowly): the royal official (desperately afraid for his son's life), the sick boy (feeling sick and scared), Jesus, the servants (who saw the boy miraculously healed).

After you "pray the miracle," tell "the rest of the story" from Focus—of the woman who was not able to climb the stairs.

> *After it became obvious that the young woman was not going to climb the stairs that night, her friends gathered around to pray some more. Some prayed for the woman to be able to walk. Some screamed at God, asking why. Some prayed to understand God's working in the young woman's life.*
>
> *Over the following years, the woman regained minimal use of her legs, but she remained unable to walk alone. But her courage and her generosity never left her. She eventually married, and adopted three children. She remained active in her church. She never lost faith that God was with her;*
> *and she lived as if she was healed.*

Suggested benediction: More than a magician, Jesus is the **GIVER OF LIFE**. Go in peace and life.

INSIGHTS FROM SCRIPTURE

A royal official came to Jesus and asked him to heal his child. This is the first opportunity in the Gospel of John for Jesus to save a life. Prior to this event, John alluded to the fact that Jesus is the "giver of life." In some ways, this event allows John to anticipate the raising of Lazarus from the dead in chapter 11.

Jesus' comment in verse 48 about "signs and wonders" is meant as something of a rebuke to the official and the crowd witnessing this exchange. Jesus does not want people to base their faith upon factual "proof" such as "signs and wonders." He wants faith in what is unseen to become real for them. Perhaps this is as much observation on the part of Jesus as it is a rebuke. For, if it had truly been a rebuke, it would have made more sense for Jesus to refuse to help the official.

The official, for his part, was not upset by Jesus' observation/rebuke. He continued to ask Jesus for help in saving his child from a sure death. The verb Jesus used in verse 50 to tell the official that his son will "live" has two meanings. On one hand, it meant that the child would survive the illness. On the other hand, John used it to refer to the idea of Jesus being the "giver of life." The child would have the life that comes through Jesus.

The official took Jesus at his word and headed home. On his way there, a servant met him and confirmed the promise Jesus made. The official's son was alive and well, and the healing came at precisely the time Jesus had spoken the words. This realization on the part of the official brought the entire household to faith. The phrase "he and his household" is not often found in John, but sounds more like the Gentile conversions found in Acts. The man believed not only in Jesus' word to heal his child, but he learned to believe in Jesus himself as the Messiah.

›› DOING VERSUS BEING

This story raises questions about the relationship between faith and healing, or signs. This is central to John's message. If someone chooses to see a miracle solely as a miraculous act and nothing else, they will become focused on, and limited to, a faith based on physical evidence. This is what Jesus warned against in his observation/rebuke in verse 48. Water turned into wine, a sick boy healed, feeding many with little are all incredible miraculous events, but they exist only in a specific time. Still, this type of miracle belies Jesus' concern for physical well-being. To look for miracles as proof of God is to say, "Look at what Jesus can do!" when we should instead be saying, "Look at who Jesus is!" He is the Giver of gifts (John 2:1-11); the Giver of life (John 4:46-53).

It is God's presence in Jesus' acts that makes them become signs, pointing to something beyond the miraculous act itself. God's presence in the acts of Jesus holds together the physical and the spiritual. It is evidence that Jesus is the "Word made flesh." Through Jesus, the fullness of God is made available to us humans, if we are able to see the visible pointing to the invisible.

For the royal official, these signs provided an opening for faith through the physical act of healing. The miracle isn't the thing, it's the vision of the presence of God working in our world that is convicting. It acknowledges the truth that "the Word became flesh and dwelt among us."

Perspective

There was once a warrior who had a fine black stallion.
Everyone said he was lucky to have such a wonderful horse.
"Maybe," the warrior said.

One day the stallion ran away.
And everyone said the warrior was unlucky.
"Maybe," the warrior said.

The next day, the stallion returned leading a string of fine ponies.
People said he was lucky.
"Maybe," the warrior said.

But the warrior's son got thrown from one of the ponies, and broke his leg.
The next week, the chief led a war party against another tribe and many young men were lost.
But the warrior's son, who had to stay behind because of his broken leg, was spared.

Permission is granted to photocopy this handout for use with this session.

SESSION 4

DANCING ON THE WATER

KEY VERSES

When they had rowed about three or four miles, they saw Jesus walking on the sea and coming near the boat, and they were terrified. But he said to them, "It is I; do not be afraid." (John 6:19-20)

FAITH STORY

John 6:16-21

FAITH FOCUS

When Jesus came walking on the rough water toward their boat in the middle of the sea, the disciples were completely shocked. They didn't know what to make of this "sign." But Jesus did not appear on the water in order to frighten the disciples. He appeared in order to calm their fears in the wind, to allow for their safe passage, and to remind them that God was, is, and always will be their rescue.

SESSION GOAL

Encourage participants to look for signs of God's presence in our world today in order to overcome fear.

Materials needed and advance preparation

- Ink blots or crayon blots (*Option A* in Focus)
- Writing paper/pencils
- Chalkboard/chalk or newsprint/marker
- Copies of the handout sheet for Session 4
- Bibles

TEACHING PLAN

1. FOCUS 10-12 minutes

Option A: Before the meeting, take several pieces of blank writing paper and place some ink in the middle of them. Fold the paper in half, thus creating ink blots. Open the paper and allow the blots to dry. You can also do this with crayon shavings—shave pieces of crayon onto a blank sheet of paper, lay another sheet on top, and then press with a hot iron to create blots of color. Make about four or five blots, and number the papers.

As your meeting begins, give participants the "ink blot" (or crayon blot) test. Give them all paper and pencils, and ask them to number their papers to 4 or 5 (however many blot papers you made) and write down whatever they happen to see in the blots. Have everyone share what they saw, jotting responses for each blot on a chalkboard or newsprint.

>>> There are multiple YouTube and Science Channel videos that go behind the scenes to discover <u>**How Did They Do That?**</u> The question "<u>how?</u>" is not John's question, though. For John, the miracles/signs are not a question of "<u>how</u>" (it is <u>God</u>, after all, so the point is moot!), but "<u>why</u>". If John can get his readers to ask <u>why</u> God did that, he anticipates that the answer will lead them to a discovery of who Jesus is and what the nature of God is.

Encourage them to have some fun with this. Assure them that their test results will not be printed in the Sunday bulletin, and no one will be forced to visit your local mental health facility, no matter how bizarre their answers may be. Most likely, no one will see the same things in every blot. The point is to explore the variety of perspectives.

>> **Option B (for outdoors):** Take everyone outside and have them lie down in a grassy area, and watch cloud shapes change. (Remember doing this as a kid?) What shapes do they see? How easy or hard is it to see the shapes that another person sees? What about looking at the cloud from a different angle? Do things look different then?

>> **Option C:** Floating finger. Have each person put their forefingers together directly in front of their eyes, so the tips touch. Now have them look *beyond* their fingers; by doing so, they should be able to see a "third" little finger. If they allow a little gap between the tips of their fingers, that third finger will appear to "float." It all depends on perspective!

2. CONNECT 5-8 minutes

Look at the variety of responses you've gotten with regard to the blots or cloud shapes, or the "success" in seeing the "floating finger." Discuss how perspective makes different people see the same thing different ways.

3. EXPLORE THE BIBLE 12-15 minutes

Shift to this activity by saying: *Rarely do all of us see things in the same way. Different perspectives can mean the difference between witnessing a sign of God's presence, or shrugging your shoulders and walking on.*

Manuscript study. On the handout sheet is the story of Jesus walking on the water, John 6:16-21, only it has no numerals or titles. Participants may be able to draw out new themes and nuances when freed from the traditional organization or printed comments. Distribute copies of the handout sheet and pencils, and ask people to read the story there and jot down at least three observations or reactions or questions at the bottom of the page. Allow at least 5 minutes. Before you share observations, tell this joke:

Three anglers rowed out into a lake for some early morning fishing. When they'd gotten out into the middle of the lake, the first one said with surprise, "Oh my! I left my hooks on the shore." She promptly stepped out of the boat and walked on top of the water to the shore. The third was speechless with amazement. Not long after the first angler had returned to the boat, the second one exclaimed, "Well, I'll be! I left my bait on the shore." She, too, stepped out of the boat and walked to the shore on top of the water. The third was shocked and terrified. When the second angler returned, the third realized, "I've left my net on the shore!" and stepped out of the boat and sank to the bottom of the lake. Just before he came back up, the first angler turned to the second and said, "Do you think we should tell him about the rocks?"

Have anyone who will do so share observations/questions/reactions to their study of the passage on the handout sheet. Here are more questions to follow up:

1. *Do you know if this story appears anywhere else in the Gospels?* (Give them a chance to look it up in their Bibles or on the Internet.)

Answer: It appears in both Matthew (14:22-32) and Mark (6:45-51).

2. *Check out the other two stories, as well as this one in John. What event happens just before the walking on water in each instance?*

Answer: A feeding miracle. This would imply that the feeding miracle and Jesus walking on water were linked in the early Christian tradition of telling these stories.

> 3. *What might be the purpose of this miracle? Why would Jesus bother to walk on water?*

Answer: First, see what insights the participants come up with. One possibility was for Jesus to show the disciples once again that it is not what he does, but *who he is* that they should be seeing. He had just performed a great miracle in feeding all of these people. They had seen a physical act beyond imagination. But that is not all Jesus wanted them (and us) to see.

For the Jews, water symbolized the forces of chaos, or evil. For Jesus to walk on top of the water means that he has conquered the powers of chaos, and is, therefore, divine. No person, not a magician or a wonder-worker, can conquer chaos. Only God can do that. So for the disciples to see Jesus walking on top of the water, they saw that Jesus had conquered the powers of evil and placed them under his feet.

4. APPLY 10 minutes

Remind participants that Jesus did not appear on the water in order to frighten the disciples. He appeared in order to **calm their fears** in the wind, to allow for their safe passage, and to remind them that God was, is, and always will be their rescue.

Now get into pairs, and share with partners:

> 1. **Childhood bedtime fears.** *What is the monster that lived under your bed? That lived behind the closet door? Or what other childhood fear did you have?* After each person has shared, ask them to face their fears by considering:
>
> 2. What kind of sign would they need for reassurance that God is there with them?

You as leader could start with a story of your own. For example: *I used to imagine that there was a two-headed green thing with spindly, snakey arms that would grab my feet if I ever stuck them out from under the covers. What kind of sign would I need to alleviate that fear? I'd want God to board up the underbed!* or *I'd want God to shine a flashlight under there to show me the monster was gone.*

5. RESPOND 8-10 minutes

Move to your "prayer closet" area.

Pray the miracle. First, ask participants to close their eyes and try to see themselves in each of the characters of the story (go slowly): the disciples (tired from struggling in the storm and getting nowhere); Jesus (coming to calm them down and instead terrifying his friends); again the disciples (as they recognized Jesus on the water). Do you dare ask them to imagine being the boat tossed on the waves? The sea that threatened to swamp the boat?

Pray also that God's power might be made real to us. This is a bit like praying to be struck by lightning. Even though it is frightening to pray such a prayer (or at least it should be), it is also a great gift. The disciples experienced a display of the power of God that night on the water. God promises us that we can experience such displays, if we have the courage to see them.

Suggested benediction: God was, is, and always will be your rescue. Go in peace.

DIFFERENT PERSPECTIVE

- A rainbow

- The differentially refracted electromagnetic radiation in the Earth's atmosphere.

Simply two different descriptions for the same thing. Depends on your perspective.

LOOK AHEAD

For a memorable experience of the story of the raising of Lazarus next session, allow a small piece of meat to "go bad," getting really stinky. You can speed up the process by tenderizing it (pounding it), which breaks down cells and allows enzymes to escape and begin to decay the meat. Tuck some spray air freshener in with this goody bag!

For an alternative, gather herbs and spices for embalming (*Option C* in Focus), along with bowls, spoons, and a hotplate. You will also need to ask a good reader in your group to prepare an expressive reading of John 11:1-44.

Other supplies include five pennies for each person, string or yarn or masking tape, 12-20 medium-sized plastic garbage bags, and two identical flat-topped tables (*Option B* in Apply).

INSIGHTS FROM SCRIPTURE

The image of Jesus walking on the water must have been an extremely powerful moment of God's revelation for the disciples. Three of the four Gospels record it (John, Matthew, and Mark). For this event to have been recorded by three different writers indicates it was very important to the early followers of the Way.

This miracle is linked to the feeding miracle. Jesus met physical needs when he fed the crowd. That feeding was a part of why Jesus came to us—to meet physical needs. The walking on water met something of a spiritual need in the disciples. They needed to be fed with the knowledge that Jesus had the same power God has, because Jesus *is* God incarnate (in the flesh).

John, unlike Matthew and Mark, does not try to explain the disciples' fear at seeing Jesus. Jesus is not a ghost or a spirit. The reason for the disciples' fear is simple—they are shocked at actually being allowed to view the divine. Jesus is God, and that revelation scared them speechless.

But Jesus knew their fear. He knew they saw him and were terrified. The NRSV and the NIV Bibles translate Jesus' words as "It is I...." This is one way to translate this passage. It is also translated as "I AM...." Sound familiar? It would have to his disiples. This is the way God identified himself to Moses at the burning bush when Moses wanted to know who was sending him to free the Israelites. "I AM" is considered to be one of the divine names of God (Hebrew: Yahweh). For Jesus to have said such a thing was to proclaim openly exactly who he really is.

The second part of Jesus' statement to the disciples in the passage also identifies Jesus: "Do not be afraid" is the standard response of God and the angels when they visit humans. In both testaments of the Bible, when a divine appearance happens, some of the first words spoken by the one appearing are: "Do not be afraid."

These two statements together create a powerful pronouncement on the part of Jesus. Jesus is God. He has said it. It cannot be taken back or changed. Such powerful words cannot be altered once they are spoken.

DID HE WALK ON WATER?

A question we all like to ask is, *Did Jesus actually walk on the water?* From the way John used the Greek language, he meant to say that Jesus was clearly walking on the water, not the shore. In other places in John, it is said that Jesus was walking on the shore, and those passages differ in their grammar from this one. Although it still does not explain *how* Jesus walked on the water, it would appear that John wants to say clearly that Jesus was *on* the water, not the shore.

There are multiple YouTube and Science Channel videos that go behind the scenes to discover *How Did They Do That?* The question—*how?*—is not John's question, though. For John, the miracles/signs are not a question of *how* (it is *God*, after all, so the point is moot!), but *why*. If John can get his readers to ask *why* God did that, he anticipates that the answer will lead them to a discovery of who Jesus is and what the nature of God is.

There is another notable feature to this passage. It is the only place in John where the disciples are said to be *frightened* by Jesus. This event was so shocking to them that John felt it necessary to make special note of the fear the disciples experienced in the face of God. Jesus does not appear on the water in order to frighten the disciples. In fact, it is much the opposite. He appears in order to calm their fears in the wind, to allow for their safe passage, and to remind them that God was, is, and always will be their rescue. This is a moment of pastoral care by Jesus for the disciples' sake.

When evening came, Jesus' disciples went down to the sea, got into a boat, and started across the sea to Capernaum. It was now dark, and Jesus had not yet come to them. The sea became rough because a strong wind was blowing. When they had rowed about three or four miles, they saw Jesus walking on the sea and coming near the boat, and they were terrified. But he said to them, "It is I; do not be afraid." Then they wanted to take him into the boat, and immediately the boat reached the land toward which they were going.

Do Miracles Happen? : Session 4

 If you think this miracle story could use a title, what would it be?

DIFFERENT PERSPECTIVE

- A rainbow
- The differentially refracted electromagnetic radiation in the Earth's atmosphere.

Simply two different descriptions for the same thing. Depends on your perspective.

 Permission is granted to photocopy this handout for use with this session.

>>> **SESSION 5**

LOOKING FOR RESURRECTION >>>

>>> KEY VERSE

When Jesus heard [that Lazarus was ill], he said, "This illness does not lead to death; rather it is for God's glory, so that the Son of God may be glorified through it." (John 11:4)

>>> FAITH STORY

John 11:1-44

>>> FAITH FOCUS

When his good friend became ill and near death, Jesus nevertheless stayed away until it was too late. Lazarus was dead before Jesus arrived, and the grieving sisters, Martha and Mary, took Jesus to task about his tardiness. Jesus assured the women that Lazarus would rise again. Even though Lazarus had been in the grave for four days, Jesus called him from death, and he came out of the tomb. This miracle of resurrection not only pointed to Jesus as the author of resurrection and life, but also foreshadowed his own death and resurrection.

>>> SESSION GOAL

Teach participants to redirect their prayers for miracles to prayers for understanding of how God is glorified in everyday events of resurrection.

TEACHING PLAN

>>> Materials needed and advance preparation

- Allow a small piece of meat to "go bad," get really stinky (*Option A* in Focus)
- Spray air freshener (*Option A* in Focus)
- String, yarn, or masking tape (*Option B* in Focus)
- Bowls, spoons, hotplate (*Option C* in Focus)
- Variety of herbs and spices (*Option C* in Focus)
- Ask a good reader in your group to prepare an expressive reading of John 11:1-44
- Bibles
- Copies of the handout sheet for Session 5
- Five pennies for each person; metal can
- Two identical flat-topped tables (*Option B* in Apply)
- Twelve to twenty medium-sized plastic garbage bags (*Option B* in Apply)

1. FOCUS 3-10 minutes

>>> **Option A:** *Smell of death.* Let your piece of meat "gone bad" stink up your meeting place. If this is just too distasteful, go outside and invite each person to take a whiff. When the group comments and complains, let them squirm awhile, then cover up the odor. Spray some air freshener! Move right to Connect, **Option A**, below.

Note: You can speed up the process of letting your meat decay by tenderizing it (pounding it), which breaks cells and allows enzymes to escape and begin the decaying process. Or try boiling a piece of liver in a pot of water, then not refrigerating it. It should be positively "ripe" a day or two later.

In Real Life | Do Miracles Happen? 33

>> **Option B:** Mummy Me Relay. Divide the group into at least two groups of 5-6. The first person in line must use string, yarn, or masking tape to "mummify" the next person; they must wrap and *unwrap* before the "mummy" turns and "mummifies" the next person in line. Of course, first team finished wins.

Continue with **Option B** in Connect, below.

>> **Option C:** Mix embalming spices. Embalming is most likely religious in origin, conceived as a means of preparing the dead for the life after death. Ancient embalming methods consisted of removal of the brains and viscera, and the filling of bodily cavities with a mixture of balsamic herbs and other substances. The Egyptians immersed the body in carbonate of soda, injected the arteries and veins with balsams, filled the cavities of the torso with bituminous and aromatic substances and salt, and wound cloths saturated with similar materials around the body. The Assyrians used honey in embalming, the Persians used wax, and the Jews used spices and aloes. Alexander the Great was embalmed with honey and wax.

Provide a table with bowls, spoons, and a variety of herbs and spices so participants can devise their own "embalming" recipes. You could even provide a hotplate for mixing, as some spices will change with heat. Divide into groups of two (can also be done individually), and then you "judge" the recipes/concoctions, like at a fair. The best "mixtures" could be given away or used in a children's story about Lazarus or the role of the women at Jesus' tomb.

Continue with **Option A** in Connect, below.

2. CONNECT 10 minutes

>> **Option A:** Have participants discuss what they think happens when a person dies. What evidence or reasons do they have for their thoughts? Let them tell stories of near-death and after-death experiences.

>> **Option B:** Follow up the mummy theme by pointing out a few "mummy facts":

- Burying the dead was of religious concern in Egypt, and Egyptian funeral rituals and equipment eventually became the most elaborate the world has ever known.
- Besides being embalmed (so the body could still be available if needed in the afterlife), Egyptian mummies were accompanied in their tombs by personal possessions and "necessities" for the afterlife.
- Wood or stone replicas of the body were put into the tomb in the event that the mummy was destroyed. The greater the number of statue-duplicates in his or her tomb, the more chances the dead person had of resurrection.

Ask participants what objects *they'd* like to take with them when they die, if they could. Why?

3. EXPLORE THE BIBLE 12-15 minutes

Shift to this activity by saying: *Most of us have lots of questions about an afterlife. We probably wonder what resurrection is all about, too. The story of the raising of Jesus' friend Lazarus from the dead is a good place to ask such questions.*

Ahead of time, ask a good reader in your group, perhaps someone who is active in theater, to prepare an expressive reading of John 11:1-44. Let your reader proclaim the passage, then pass out Bibles and handout sheets for the discussion.

When your reader finishes, discuss (use the "answer" as part of the discussion): *Why would Martha, in verses 25-27, be able to confess who Jesus really is and get it exactly right, yet, in verse 39, she seems to deny the confession she just made?*

Answer: First, John seems to show many human beings, particularly in their interactions with Jesus, being confused. They say one thing and end up doing something very different. This could be John just highlighting how fickle we humans really are, or he could be emphasizing that no one really understood who and what Jesus really was until after the resurrection, no matter what they said. **Second**, Martha may have made a completely accurate statement in verses 25-27, and known exactly what she was saying, but when faced with the reality of opening the tomb, she forgot. In those days and in that culture, human bodies were not embalmed. Israel is a warm, desert-like atmosphere. After three days in a hot, stuffy cave, Lazarus' body would have smelled like the worst thing you can imagine. Also, according to ancient belief, a person's spirit could linger in the body for three days. Lazarus is now past that point - he is really, really dead. So Martha was voicing a practical concern, since it seemed that Lazarus really was beyond hope. Like Martha, we may confess Jesus' power, but when it comes right down to it, the sign might seem too improbable or very scary.

Also ask, *What was Jesus trying to prove by raising Lazarus in the first place? What do you think he was trying to prove by waiting until Lazarus had begun to stink?*

Answer: Think about the Madeleine L'Engle quote in the sidebar, or draw from the Insights section.

Next, pass out 5 pennies to each person. As you ask the next discussion question, have participants "commit" to their answer by dropping pennies into a metal can. Ask: *Do you believe Jesus could have actually done this in reality?* If they believe very strongly that he could, they drop all 5 pennies into the can. If they don't believe it at all, they wouldn't drop any. Other participants may put in more or fewer pennies, depending on how strongly sure they feel about whether Jesus could have raised someone from the dead. Have participants come forward all at one time, then shake the can and open the question for discussion. Add this "answer" to the discussion if you like:

Answer: The truth is that this is strictly a personal faith issue. Either you are open to believing Jesus performed miracles, or you aren't. There isn't much room for a middle ground. It's chickening out to say you believe in some of the miracles that Jesus is reported to have performed and not others. It is also not fair to depend completely on the answers of scholars, either. They weren't there any more than you were. You either must be open or not.

4. APPLY 8-10 minutes

>> **Option A:** Now assign participants the task to search their room **in silence** (go outside, if possible, or expand the search to other rooms if appropriate) for everyday things that might symbolize resurrection. Examples (in case some feel stuck): the earth in a flowerpot, a wooden chair (a tree died), shoe leather (an animal died), food (from a seed that underwent transformation). After about 5 minutes, call everyone to bring their item to the center of a circle. Ask each person to explain how they saw resurrection in their item.

>> **Option B (for large groups):** Using two identical flat-topped tables and medium-sized plastic garbage bags, have participants demonstrate "raising" a table using only air. Ask as many people as can possibly stand around one of the tables to stand around the table and give them each a plastic bag. Have them spread the bags

"There was a large stone in front of the tomb where Lazarus' body had been laid, and Jesus told the people to take it away. Martha, that blunt woman, put it graphically: 'Lord, by this time he stinketh.' Jesus said to her, 'Didn't I tell you that if you would believe, you would see the glory of God?' They took away the stone, and Jesus, lifting his eyes, said, 'Father, thank you for hearing me. I know that you hear me always, but I am saying this now so that the people around me may believe that you have sent me.' And he cried out with a loud voice, 'Lazarus, come forth!'"

Madeleine L'Engle,
The Glorious Impossible

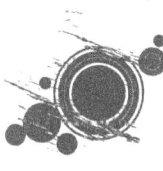

out on the table and hold the bag's mouth in their hands to get set to blow air into them (let everyone stay in a squatting position around the table). Make sure that everyone is ready to blow air into the bags with the hands and fingers away from the tabletop.

Now ask two or four other people to lift the other identical table, turn it upside down and put it slowly on the first table. Take care! It has to move over the heads of the others at the first table. Let the people squatting now blow air in the plastic bags, all together, on the count of three.

What will happen: By blowing into the plastic bags, air is being compressed. This compressed air causes the table to rise, much like pumping tires of a bike or a car. Tire pressure is two to four times as high as the atmospheric pressure. The table on top, even with the heavy weight, will rise!

Point out that in the Bible, the words for "air" or "breath" are the same as for "spirit." Just like our air caused the table to rise, when God's Spirit (breath, wind, air) is present, things can rise—Lazarus!

5. RESPOND 8-20 minutes

Move to your "prayer closet" area.

Pray the miracle. First, ask participants to close their eyes and to try to see themselves in each of the characters of the story (go slowly): the disciples (who were puzzled by Jesus' announcement that he was going "to wake up" Lazarus); Jesus (whose friend had died); Martha (who was angry that Jesus didn't come earlier); Mary (who also grieved for her dead brother); the crowd (who saw Lazarus come out of the grave). Do you dare ask them to imagine being Lazarus, who found himself alive and surrounded by staring people?

During your prayer time, encourage participants to dwell on their own birth, life, and death.

Suggested benediction: God is glorified in everyday events of resurrection. Let us keep our eyes open!

INSIGHTS FROM SCRIPTURE

The story of Jesus raising Lazarus is found only in John. John uses it to foreshadow Jesus' own death, from which he, too, will be raised to life. The other Gospels tell instead the story of Jesus raising Jarius' daughter from the dead (Matt. 9:18-26; Mark 5:21-43; Luke 8:40-56). Raising people from the dead was an integral part of early Christian stories about Jesus.

The town of Bethany mentioned in this story is very near Jerusalem. The other Gospels identify this town as the place Jesus stayed just before and during the week leading up to his crucifixion. Bethany is also associated with being the place where Mary anointed Jesus (John 11:2; 12:1-8).

>>>
"The grave seems to interrupt the human story. But the fact is that graves are motherly for the Earth. They wrap up the things of time and deliver them back to the cradle. So that the show goes on. So that nothing will stop the stories from being told . . . . The soil of graves is the transformer. It is natural magic. The grave is a memory from which the story of the Earth is told."

William Bryant Logan,
Dirt: The Ecstatic Skin of the Earth

»» WHY WAIT?

People of ancient Israel believed that when a person died, the soul of that person hung around for three days. The soul wanted a chance to get back into the body and come back into life. After three days, however, the soul would see that the color of the body's face had changed (in other words, the body was starting to decay), so it would leave and go on to the afterlife.

In verses 21 and 22, Martha complained to Jesus that if only he had been there, Lazarus would not have died. Would Martha dare complain to Jesus? It was normal, and a very important part of the Jewish faith, to be able to complain like that, even to God! Martha's complaint shows her continued confidence in Jesus' ability to do something about this situation. Lazarus may have been dead, but if anyone could do something about that problem, Martha knew it was Jesus. She may not have expected what she got, though!

Verses 25 and 26 are vital for seeing who Jesus is, and what claims he made to Martha. His statement that "I am the resurrection and the life..." upended long-held understandings of God and salvation. With these words Jesus was radically changing the idea of what the people should expect from God. He declared *himself* to be God. His question, then, was not just to Martha. It is a question to each one of us. Do we believe that Jesus is who he says he is? If we do, then we receive the promise of eternal life.

When verse 33 uses the word "disturbed" or "troubled" to describe Jesus' feelings, then verse 35 marks that Jesus wept, it makes it seem as if Jesus is also mourning over a dead man whom he has no intention of allowing to remain dead. Such a paradox makes no sense. If, on the other hand, Jesus' feeling in verse 33 is translated as "anger" or "agitation," then Jesus' tears may appropriately be considered an acknowledgment of the pain that death causes humans to experience. Jesus is feeling with us as humans, and acknowledging that our pain is real and deserves expression. As pastor Kurt Borgmann writes, "This chapter in John's gospel is really about…the glory of resurrection. It's a story about life renewed and reclaimed. But…it's as much a story about compassion and empathy and… heart. Jesus may be true to his mission…of revealing the glory of God, but…he sees and hears the weeping, the grief, the pain of life lost, and it not only disturbs him; it moves him to tears of his own."

Jesus' tears, however, do not change the fact that he intends to raise Lazarus back to life. The miracle John describes is one that clearly points to the glory of God, the Life-Giver.

»»

"Every blade in the field–every leaf in the forest–lays down its life in its season as beautifully as it was taken up."

Henry David Thoreau

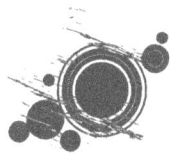

»»

"In the case of Jesus, [there are glints of resurrection life] all the time, everywhere we look: acts of compassion, clear and careful teaching, advocacy for peace, ministry to the poor, aloneness without loneliness, prophetic risks, small children welcomed, meals shared with the outcasts, the community of love. Jesus is reappearing, is resurrected all over the place."

Kurt Borgmann

Looking for Resurrection!

In Real Life — Exploring tough questions facing youth today

Listen to a reading of John 11:1-44. Then use Bibles to prepare your perspective for discussion.

1. Why would Martha, in verses 25-27, be able to confess who Jesus really is and get it exactly right, yet, in verse 39, she seems to deny the confession she just made?

2. What was Jesus trying to prove by raising Lazarus in the first place? What do you think he was trying to prove by waiting until Lazarus had begun to stink?

3. Do you believe Jesus could have actually done this?

Commit to your answer with money! If you believe very strongly that he could, drop all 5 pennies you have into the can. If you don't believe it at all, don't drop any. Put in more or fewer pennies, depending on how strongly you feel about whether Jesus could have raised someone from the dead.

>>>

"There was a large stone in front of the tomb where Lazarus' body had been laid, and Jesus told the people to take it away. Martha, that blunt woman, put it graphically: 'Lord, by this time he stinketh.' Jesus said to her, 'Didn't I tell you that if you would believe, you would see the glory of God?' They took away the stone, and Jesus, lifting his eyes, said, 'Father, thank you for hearing me. I know that you hear me always, but I am saying this now so that the people around me may believe that you have sent me.' And he cried out with a loud voice, 'Lazarus, come forth!'"

Madeleine L'Engle,
The Glorious Impossible

Do Miracles Happen? : Session 5

Permission is granted to photocopy this handout for use with this session.

⟫⟫ EXTENDER SESSION

(*Option A* best used after Session 2, *Option B* best used after Session 3)

FOLLOW THE SIGNS

⟫⟫ OPTION A

SESSION GOAL
Facilitate an opportunity for participants to live the outward signs of the Sign they follow, Jesus.

⟫⟫ PLAN
If you already know about food sharing and food security projects in your area, find a time and make plans with the organization about what how the group can plug in to help. If you aren't familiar, try an Internet search using those words and make contacts to help feed people in your community. You might also contact Catholic Charities in your diocese, or a local St. Vincent de Paul food pantry. This service project will expose the participants to some of the needs in their immediate area. Sometimes it's more exciting to serve at a distant location on service trips, neglecting the needs that are readily found in our own area.

⟫⟫ OPTION B

SESSION GOAL
Explore further the connection of faith and healing.

⟫⟫ PLAN
View the movie *Leap of Faith*, starring Steve Martin as a fake faith healing hustler who gets set on his heels when one of his healings really works. Debrief after the movie, asking participants to talk about how they felt about each of the main characters. How do they think the boy was healed? Do they think the character played by Steve Martin grew in his faith or not? Do you think God might have been present in this story? Where?

⟫⟫ Materials needed and advance preparation

- Internet connection (*Option A*)
- Media player, *Leap of Faith* movie (*Option B*)

⟫⟫

"To treat life as less than a miracle is to give up on it."

Wendell Berry

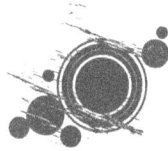

In Real Life
Exploring tough questions facing youth today

CLUELESS AND CALLED
Discipleship and the Gospel of Mark

What does it take to be a disciple? This study of the Gospel of Mark focuses on the requirements for following Jesus' way and the abundant life that is ours as a result. (5 sessions)

DO MIRACLES HAPPEN?
Signs and Wonders in the Gospel of John

The greatest miracle, recorded in John 1:14 and 3:16, is the miracle of God's love that became flesh and lived among us. But John also included examples of what we more traditionally think of as miracles: the wonder of abundance from little; healing; signs of impossibility and faith; and the resurrection. (5 sessions)

DO THE RIGHT THING
Ethics Shaped by Faith

How do you know what's right and what's wrong? Even when you figure it out, the right thing is often the unpopular or unpleasant choice. This unit offers participants a clearer sense of what it means to claim a faith identity, a foundation that can help them sort out the gritty details of ethics shaped by faith. (6 sessions)

FIGHT RIGHT
A Christian Approach to Conflict Resolution

This unit will help youth understand conflict and its function. They will learn how they can be honest and loving, and explore how conflict can be used for positive results. They will also learn ways to enhance their communication skills. 1 Corinthians. (5 sessions)

GOD IS A WARRIOR?
Violence in the Bible

The Bible challenges us to be reconciled to one another and work for justice. So what do we do with the stories that seem to condone violence or even encourage it? A discussion of issues in the Old and New Testaments. (6 sessions)

HOW DO YOU KNOW?
Wisdom in the Bible

Wisdom literature teaches us that we gain knowledge of the world, ourselves, and God through experience and observation. This unit provides practical, hands-on wisdom to help young people avoid life's snares and grow closer to God. Proverbs, Job, Ecclesiastes. (5 sessions)

HOW TO BE A TRUE FRIEND
The Bible Reveals Friendship's Heart

To be a friend takes skill. Help youth discover the secrets of friendship through various stories from the Old and New Testament. (6 sessions)

HOW TO READ THE BIBLE
Building Skills for Bible Study

What kind of book is the Bible? What does this book mean to me? This unit looks at the Bible as revelation, as history, as literature. Selected scripture. (5 sessions)

KEEPING THE GARDEN
A Faith Response to God's Creation

If Christians believe that God made the world, we do not need any more compelling reason to care for it than that God has handed us a treasure to hold and protect. This unit gets beyond trendy environmentalism and challenges youth to see environmental awareness as a religious issue. Genesis. (6 sessions)

MANTRAS, MENORAHS, AND MINARETS
Encountering Other Faiths

How is Christianity different from other faiths? Why do others believe the way they do? This study can give youth a new appreciation for the uniqueness of Jesus. Selected scripture. (5 sessions)

SALT, LIGHT, AND THE GOOD LIFE
The Beatitudes and the Sermon on the Mount

What can youth expect in a life of discipleship? This unit explores the Sermon on the Mount under four main sections: the Beatitudes, Salt and Light, Jesus and the Law, and Heavenly Teachings. Matthew 5. (6 sessions)

A SPECK IN THE UNIVERSE
The Bible on Self-Esteem and Peer Pressure

Discover God's unconditional love and acceptance of all people. This study will show positive ways to have one's life make a difference, and help youth find ways to resist negative peer pressure and turn it into positive action. (6 sessions)

THE RADICAL REIGN
Parables of Jesus

Jesus used parables to reveal what the kingdom of God is like, and how God relates to us. This study highlights how the parables reveal God's reign as radically different from the world we live in, and what that means for the Christian life. (6 sessions)

TESTING THE WATERS
Basic Tenets of Faith

Discover the biblical roots for the central Christian concepts of covenant, community, and baptism. This short course is a way to test the (baptismal) waters of Christianity before diving in, or review the basics for those who already have. (6 sessions)

WHO IS GOD?
Engaging the Mystery

God is beyond human comprehension, yet desires to be known. These sessions focus on the way we get clues about and glimpses of God from the Bible, God's creation, and church tradition. Selected scripture. (5 sessions)

www.ingramcontent.com/pod-product-compliance
Lightning Source LLC
Chambersburg PA
CBHW080409170426

43193CB00016B/2863